KU-662-438

MUMMY NEVER TOLD ME

Babette Cole

TED SMART

Mummy never told me that life
is full of little secrets.

BONK

Why is Mummy so busy
that she has no time for me?

Why must I go to school . . .

when Mummy was expelled from hers?

What does the tooth fairy

really look like?

QUACK!

Mummy never told me that
boys are different from girls . . .

or that
it's hard
to tell

the grown-up
ones apart!

Why do
grown-ups
have hair
in their
ears,

and up their
nostrils,

but sometimes
none on their
heads?

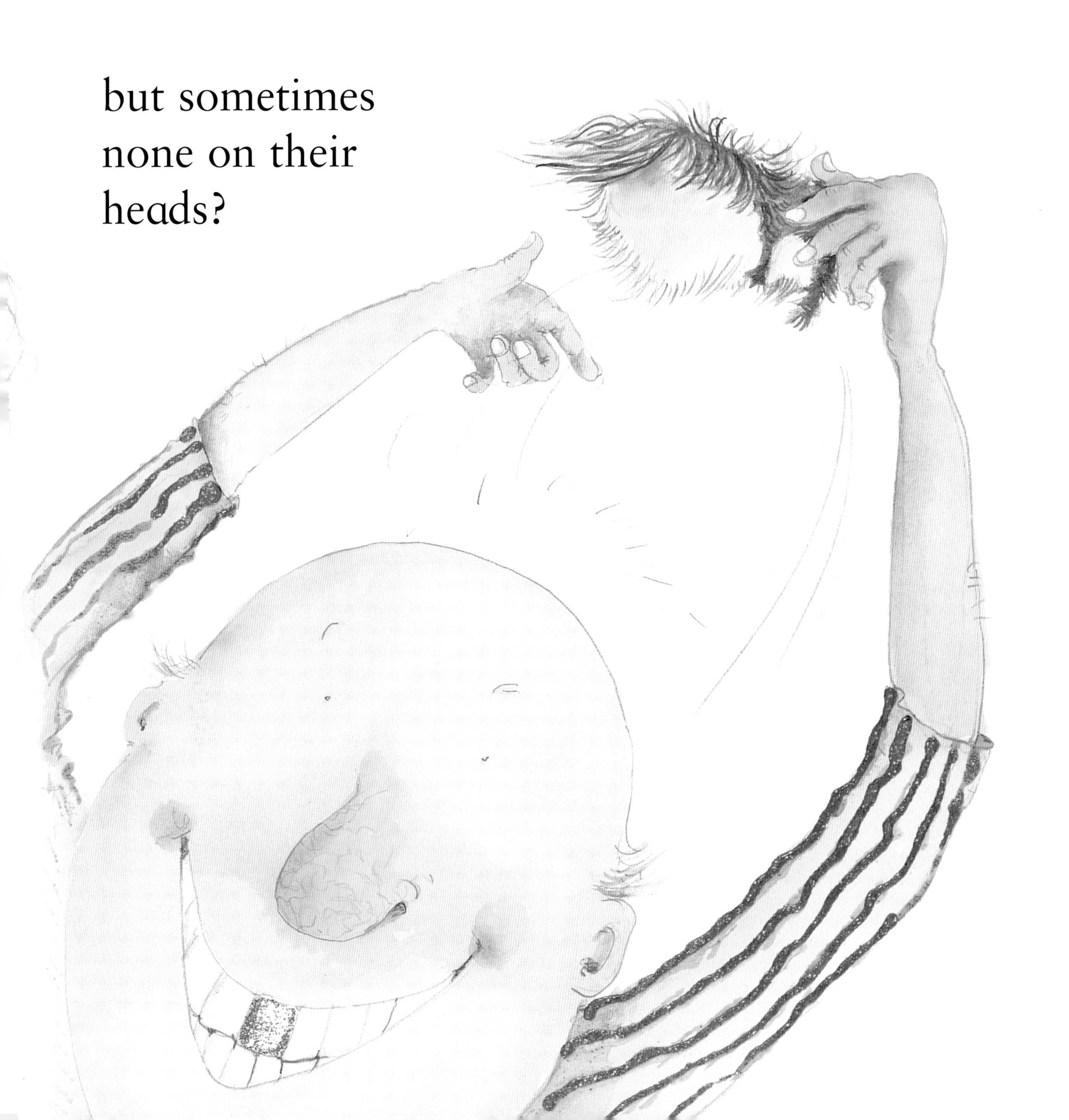

Doctors can help them
choose a new nose.

But they don't tell you what
to do with the old ones!

She didn't tell me why
some grown-ups go to sleep
with their teeth in a jar beside them,

or why they
spend so long
in the bathroom!

Why do Mummy and Daddy

lock me out of their bedroom?

Where do they go

at night?

Where do mummies and daddies
who can't have babies get one from?

How can you
hate someone . . .

and love them
at the same
time?

Why do some women prefer to fall in love with other women . . .

and some men
with other men?

But I'm not worried.
She'll tell me when the time comes!

To Boo

MUMMY NEVER TOLD ME

This edition produced for The Book People Ltd,
Hall Wood Avenue, Haydock, St Helens, WA11 9UL

First published in Great Britain by Jonathan Cape,
an imprint of Random House Children's Books

Jonathan Cape edition published 2003
The Book People edition published 2003

1 3 5 7 9 10 8 6 4 2

RANDOM HOUSE CHILDREN'S BOOKS
61–63 Uxbridge Road, London W5 5SA
A division of The Random House Group Ltd

RANDOM HOUSE AUSTRALIA (PTY) LTD
20 Alfred Street, Milsons Point, Sydney,
New South Wales 2061, Australia

RANDOM HOUSE NEW ZEALAND LTD
18 Poland Road, Glenfield, Auckland 10, New Zealand

RANDOM HOUSE (PTY) LTD
Endulini, 5A Jubilee Road, Parktown 2193, South Africa

THE RANDOM HOUSE GROUP Limited Reg. No. 954009

A CIP catalogue record for this book is available from the British Library.

Printed in Singapore